RHYMES *of* THE HEART

RHYMES *of* THE HEART

POETRY IN MOTION

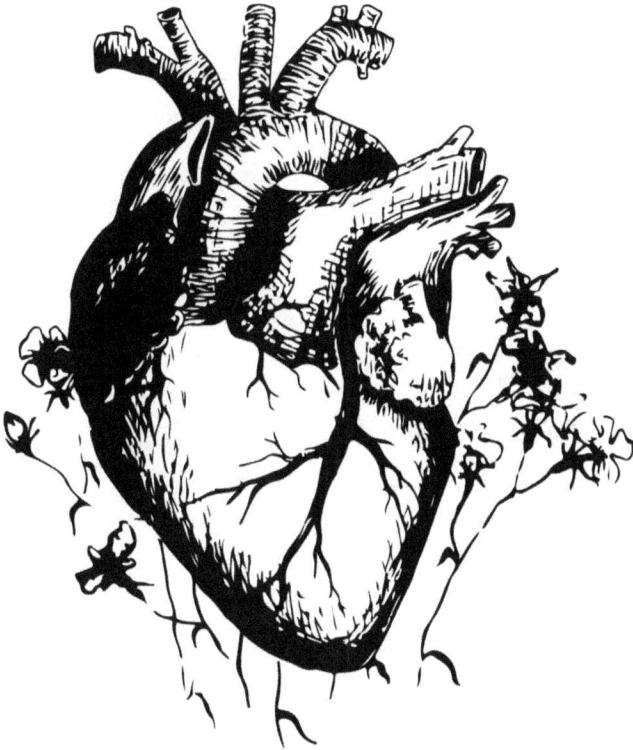

Written by
Fathmath Sheena

RHYMES OF THE HEART
Poetry in Motion

Wipf & Stock
An Imprint of Wipf and Stock Publishers
199 W. 8th Ave., Suite 3
Eugene, OR 97401

www.wipfandstock.com

PAPERBACK ISBN: 979-8-3852-1838-7
HARDCOVER ISBN: 979-8-3852-1839-4
EBOOK ISBN: 979-8-3852-1840-0

In Loving Memory of My Mother

To the guardian of my dreams and the inspiration behind my words – my mother, this book is for you.

Mariyam Abdullah
1967 - 2023

AUTHOR'S NOTE

This collection of poems delves into the depths of grief, the complexities of pain, and the power of hope. Each verse is carefully woven with words that seek to shine a light on the often misunderstood landscape of mental health.

Through introspection and vulnerability, my aim is to inspire and motivate, reminding you that

feeling pain is a part of being human.

These poems serve as a gentle reminder that you are not alone in your struggles. I aim to cultivate a sense of unity, encouraging dialogue and understanding surrounding mental health awareness. Even in the darkest moments, there is always a glimmer of hope at the end of the tunnel, a ray of light that guides you towards healing and renewal.

May these verses provide solace and ignite a flame within your heart, reminding you that you have the strength to overcome, to rise above the challenges that life presents.

Embrace the journey, for within the rhymes of the heart lies the power to heal and transform.

With love & hope,
f.sheena

In rhymes of the heart, I find my art.
In words I weave, my emotions unfold.

YOU
MATTER

Mental health matters, let's weave compassion
into life's chapters.

My Mother

Your love is like a guiding star,
Leading me through life's treacherous bars.
Now that you're gone, the world feels so cold.
And my days are like a story untold.

Our last memories, in hospital beds we lay,
But you, my mother, were so brave in every way.
The pain you endured, never once you complain,
In your strength, forever you shall remain.

On your death bed, you shone so bright,
Radiant and strong, no matter the fight.
I held your hand as you took your last breath.
Kissed your beautiful face, so peaceful in death.

Tears flowed freely down my cheeks,
As I embraced you with love that never weaks.
My heart heavy with grief, yet full of pride,
For the courage you showed till the very last ride.

You've faced countless life challenges, that's true,
Yet you shielded me, so strong and true.
With all your heart, you cared for me,
More than for yourself, right from the very start.

You are so beautiful, my mother.
Your dark hair and brown eyes like no other.
You have the best smile in the world,
And in my heart, you will forever be swirled.

— 99 —

As you navigate the depths of grief, may you find solace in the enduring power of your mother's love, a source of strength that will guide you through even the darkest of nights.

Sorrow's Fire: A Warrior's Battle

The burning ache within her chest,
It feels so real, so deeply pressed.
Silent screams, they fill her head,
Loneliness surrounds her like a bed.

She don't feel like she can be saved,
The pain too real, too deeply engraved.
Loss that words cannot describe,
She's faking smiles, she's living a lie.

Her beauty hides the pain she bear,
Her heart is shattered, beyond repair,
Strong and mighty they she is,
But every night she die again.

The darkness surrounds her, a constant friend,
While she give her light to others to mend.
Her heart has died, though she is alive,
How do she describe this pain that thrives?

She is not good enough, she is told,
But she keep going, she's ever so bold.
Her pain is real, though she hide it well,
She's a warrior fighting a battle from hell.

But, still the ache burns deep inside,
She'll keep fighting, though her heart has died.
Her strength will carry her through this pain,
She'll rise and learn to love again.

— 99 —

In pain, we find our hidden might, Embrace the ache, reclaim the light.

Silent battles birth warriors,
their strength a beacon for us all.

Minds, like oceans, ebb and flow,
each wave a journey, every tide a chance to grow.

EMBRACE THE JOURNEY, NO MATTER HOW TOUGH

TURN OBSTACLES INTO OPPORTUNITIES

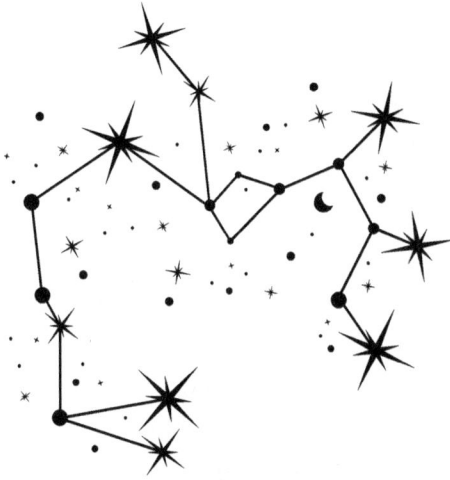

Nurture scars as constellations, mapping tales of resilience through life's revelations.

A People Pleaser's Plight

Amidst the chaos, she sits and dwells,
Mixed emotions, her own personal hell.
The world seems to be against her,
A never-ending struggle, hard to break free.

Her anxiety feeds her, dark thoughts abound,
She tries to escape, but they still surround.
She doesn't know herself, lost in her own mind,
Wishing she could be more, but struggling to find.

The world feels so dark, full of despair,
Unloved and alone, no one seems to care.
Fake smiles and forced laughter everywhere,
It's hard to believe that anyone is truly there.

Perhaps she's too hard on herself, it's true,
A people pleaser, she wants to be liked by you.
But the fear of being unwanted, it's real,
A vast audience, a constant ordeal.

So she puts on a mask, a smile on her face,
Trying to be likeable, to find her place.
But each night, she goes to bed feeling so sad,
The mask falls off, and her heart feels so bad.

Oh, how she wishes she could break free,
From the pain and the hurt, that follows her.
To find her own path, to be true to herself,
To leave behind the mask, to be someone else.

———— **99** ————

In darkness, seek the strength to rise, authenticity brings the greatest prize.

Wild and Restless Heart

In fields of gold and open skies,
She wanders free with fearless eyes.
A wild and restless spirit,
Her heart with love does overflow.

With each new day, she takes to flight,
Her heart ablaze with pure delight.
A soft lover, tender and true,
Her passion burns like morning dew.

In fields of green and azure blue,
She dances with the morning dew.
Her soul so pure, so full of light,
Her love, a flame that burns so bright.

Through forest paths and winding lanes,
Her heart beats wild, without restrain.
A wild wanderer, she roams free,
Her heart a beacon, for all to see.

Her laughter echoes through the air,
A song of joy, so sweet and rare.
A soft lover, with a heart so true,
Her love, a gift, for me and you.

And when the night comes, she rests her head,
Her soul at peace, her heart well-fed.
A wild wanderer, a soft lover,
A heart so full, it overflows forever.

———— 99 ————

Unleash the wild heart within you, roam free without restraint. Welcome the tender passion of a soft lover, embody the spirit of fearlessness.

Embrace your pain.
It's the human touchstone.

YOU CAN CONQUER AND TRANSFORM

The Depths of Rescue

In the deep blue sea, she was drowning,
The waters filled her lungs, no air left for breathing.
She fought with all her might, but the waves kept her down,
She screamed so loud, but the sound didn't make a sound.

Her heart pounded, her mind raced,
As she struggled to break free from the watery embrace.
She looked around, but there was no one in sight,
No one to hear her cries, no one to share her fright.

As the darkness closed in, and her vision grew dim,
She thought of all the things she'd never get to see again.
Her family, her friends, the places she'd been,
All of them now just memories, never to be seen.

She prayed for a miracle, for someone to rescue her,
But the only thing she got was the cold and endless sea.
She felt so alone, so helpless, and afraid,
As she sank deeper and deeper, into water's cold embrace.

But just as she thought it was the end of her life,
A glimmer of light shone through the water, piercing the night.
It grew closer and brighter, until she could see,
A hand reaching out, reaching for her.

With one last burst of strength, she reached out to grasp,
And the hand pulled her up from the depths at last.
As she gasped for air, and the world came back into view,
She knew that she owed her life to the stranger who pulled her through.

*Remember, even in profound depths, there's unseen help,
and salvation can be found.*

A Dream of Breaking Chains

In the still of night, she lies awake,
With a heart full of doubt and a soul that aches.
She battles anxiety, a fierce foe indeed.
And the weight of self-judgment, a heavy burden to heed.

But in her eyes, there's a glimmer of light,
A hope that shines through the darkest of night.
She whispers to herself, "I forgive you, my dear,
And I forgive myself, I have nothing to fear".

Her chains start to break, as if by magic spell,
The weight on her chest begins to quell.
She breathes in pure, free air and then,
Begins to see the beauty that surrounds her again.

The stars above, they twinkle and dance,
As if to say, "Take a chance, take a chance".
The moon, it glows, so warm and bright,
Guiding her through the shadows of the night.

And in this moment, she's no longer alone,
For her heart and soul, they've found a new home.
A place of peace, a place of grace,
Where love and forgiveness are woven in its embrace.

So let her dreams take wing, to soar and to roam,
For in this world, she's found a new home.
A place where she can be her truest self,
And let go of the chains that bound her to hell.

—————— **99** ——————

*Even in the darkest hours, forgiveness and self-love hold
the key to freedom. In freedom's dance, find peace and
grace and let your dreams take flight.*

DON'T STOP UNTIL YOU'RE PROUD

Darkness
carves
space
for
stars
of
hope,
each
twinkle
a
victory.

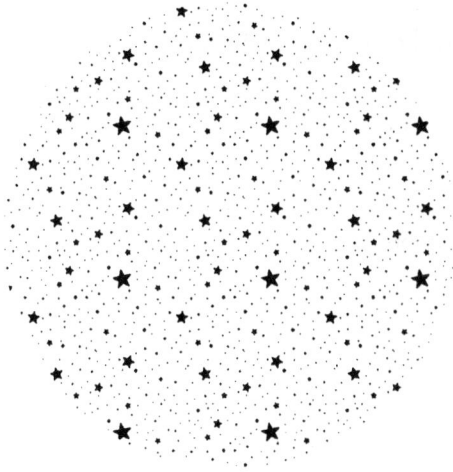

Amidst
fragmented
stars
within,
we
discover
galaxies
of
strength.

23

The Seed of Self-Love

In the misty fields of her heart's deepest desires,
Where the moonbeams dance and the stars inspire,
She discovered a truth, a secret hidden so well,
That not even the wind's whispers could tell.

It was the day he walked away, a distant memory now,
But back then, it was a storm that tore her apart, somehow.
Yet, in the eye of that hurricane, a seed was sown,
A seed that bloomed in her when she was alone.

It was the seed of self-love, a precious gift so rare,
That grew in the garden of her soul with gentle care.
She tended to it with kindness, watered it with her tears,
And watched it blossom in the face of her fears.

It was the beginning of a new dawn, a surreal light,
That shone upon her path in the dark of the night.
And with each step she took, the dream became more real,
The magic of her journey, the hope that she could heal.

So she danced to the melody of her heart,
And let her spirit soar, never to depart.
For the journey that began with his goodbye,
Has led her to a place where dreams can never die.

And she is grateful, beyond words could ever express,
For the pain that led her to this place of happiness.
So thank you, my love, for not wanting me,
For it was the beginning of the greatest love story.

———— **99** ————

From heartache springs strength.
Within the depths of loss lies the seed of self-love.
Celebrate the journey, for it leads to the most
extraordinary love story.

The Strength of a Thousand Deaths

In the moonlight's shimmering hue,
A girl with eyes that softly renew.
Has lived a life both dark and bright,
And seen the world with second sight.

She's danced through a thousand deaths, you see,
And lived to tell her tale to me.
For with each loss, she found new might,
A power that soared with lunar light.

Her soul is bathed in stardust's light,
A tapestry of dreams at night.
With every thread a story told,
of how she rose up bold and bold.

Her heart's a flame that flickers bright,
A beacon shining through the night.
For though she's walked through shadowed paths,
Her spirit's risen from the ash.

So let her dance in fairy rings,
And feel the magic that it brings,
For she's a dreamer, through and through,
With hope and wonder ever new.

She may have died a thousand times,
And seen the world through broken rhymes.
But every step has led her here,
A dreamer who has conquered fear.

—— 99 ——

Embrace life's phases like the moon.
Dance through darkness and gain strength from loss.
You're a dreamer, embody your magic!

Through storms of the mind,

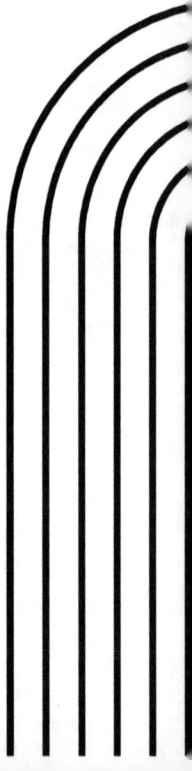

we find the strength to paint our own rainbows.

Beyond Mortal Eye

In the depths of her soul, a hidden tale unfolds,
A whispered story of battles fought, untold.
Scars etched upon her skin, like ink on a page,
But the world glances past, unable to gauge.

Just like the stars that twinkle up high,
Her journey remains veiled, beyond mortal eye.
For who comprehends the cosmic expanse,
of light traversing vast distances, in a cosmic dance?

From tender youth, she wore the weight of age,
A burden bestowed, an early life on life's stage.
Forced to confront the trials, fierce and dire,
Her innocence snatched by a cruel, relentless fire.

In shadows she resides, seeking refuge from the pain,
The trauma, a tempest she cannot fully contain.
A smile adorns her visage in the realm of the virtual,
Yet tears cascade behind the veiled curtain, so surreal.

If only one could glimpse the truth she conceals,
The unspoken anguish her heart, silently reveals.
But if you look a little closer, beyond the facade,
The cracks emerge, where her spirit is awed.

Oh, the weight of her thoughts, a heavy shroud,
Draining colors from her world, leaving whispers aloud.
Yet, amidst the darkness, a dreamy light remains,
A flicker of hope, where solace may yet be gained.

Look beyond facades, unveil the unseen, embrace kindness, for shared understanding fosters healing's embrace.

Whispers in Moonlit Trails

She's always on the run, but she doesn't know what from,
A restless soul, seeking relief, in dreams yet to come.
In her heart's labyrinth, mysteries unfurl,
Whispers of the wind, enticing her to twirl.

Through fields of lavender, she dances in grace,
Chasing fleeting shadows, in an endless chase.
The moonlight, her guide, casting a silver gleam,
A celestial compass, guiding her dreams.

In the depths of her eyes, a world begins to bloom,
Where fantasies and realities find their own room.
She treads upon moonbeams, a delicate flight,
Cloaked in stardust, she embraces the night.

She chases after whispers, trailing a moonlit haze,
Through emerald forests and ethereal maze.
The secrets of the universe whisper in her ear,
As she spins in the cosmos, void of all fear.

She yearns for answers, beneath a starry dome,
For the whispers of her soul to find a celestial home.
She dances with moonlight, as it kisses her skin,
An ethereal waltz, where dreams and reality blend.

So she'll keep on running, through nights and through days,
Chasing elusive phantoms in their mystical ways.
For in the depths of her being, a fire forever burns,
A seeker of truth, until the world's secrets she learns.

Dance with whispers, chase dreams' delight, under moonlit trails, find insight. Welcome the unknown, let spirit soar, in cosmic dance, forever explore.

A whisper of kindness to the soul can mend wounds unseen,
reminding us that compassion is a balm for the heart.

YOUR DEDICATION TODAY WILL BE YOUR SUCCESS TOMORROW

Rebirth in the Moon's Embrace

In the moonlit haze of memories past,
Where whispers of pain and sorrow last.
A soul, once vibrant, now walks alone,
In the labyrinth of a heart overthrown.

"Maybe," the stars whispered in the night,
"You are not healing, for you seek the light.
Of yesteryears, before the storm,
But new blooms await, a rebirth to transform."

A butterfly, once trapped in a chrysalis tight,
Now yearns to soar on zephyrs of flight.
But clinging to what once was known,
She fears to embrace the strength she's grown.

Yet, in the tender embrace of twilight's glow,
A gentle voice stirs, like a stream's soft flow,
"Let go of the past, my dear,
For healing blooms from acceptance clear."

Unfurl your wings, embrace the change,
Let the winds of time your essence rearrange.
For in the depth of each scar and mark,
Resides the strength to mend and spark.

Embrace the journey, the jagged and the serene,
In every fragment, a new self can be seen,
The night may seem long, but a dawn will rise,
With healing anew, beneath painted skies.

99

From pain to strength, a rebirth awaits.
Unfurl your wings, fly, and welcome the new dawn.

Beyond the Trauma: A Blossoming Soul

In the depths of wounded souls, a truth unwinds,
Whispered softly as time intertwines.
Maybe healing eludes, for we yearn to reclaim,
The innocence lost, our former selves to name.

But within these broken pieces, a tale unrolls,
A journey of resilience, where new strength molds.
For the heart's true healing lies not in rewind,
But in embracing the scars, a transformation kind.

Oh, weary loner, let the past gently fade,
Release the need to dwell in shadows that cascade.
For the trauma's touch may linger, a haunting touch,
But it's in becoming anew, we find love's clutch.

The path to healing lies in the present's embrace,
Where acceptance reigns, casting off the mask we chase.
Embrace the growth, the evolving melody of your being,
And witness the blossoms of a soul forever freeing.

You are not the same, nor should you be,
For the trials endured have forged a soul, wild and free.
So, release the chains that hold you in bygone grasp,
Embrace the unknown, a future where dreams will clasp.

In the canvas of life, woven with threads of pain,
Let resilience and hope be the colors that remain.
And as you soar on wings unfurled, radiant and true,
You'll discover healing's whisper, beckoning to you.

—— **99** ——

From scars, strength's tale blooms and resilience finds power.
Release the past's grip. Heal, transform, and rise.

Scars tell tales of battles fought,
each mark a testament to our survival.

EVERY SETBACK IS A SETUP FOR A COMEBACK

Embracing the Dance of Forgetting

In the tender realm where memories reside,
A whispered truth awaits, to gently confide.
"You will forget everything with time," they say,
As fleeting moments slip, like sand from a bay.

The weight of sorrows, burdens of the past,
Shall dissolve, like shadows that never last.
Through the corridors of moments that fade,
A new dawn emerges, where healing is made.

The ache of heartbreak, once fierce and profound,
Shall soften, like a melody's gentle sound.
For time, like a river, carves paths anew,
Washing away fragments of pain we once knew.

The wounds that seared, leaving scars unseen,
Shall heal in the embrace of the timeless serene.
With each passing hour, memories wane,
Transformed by the whispers of a forgetful terrain.

Yet, amidst the fading, a beauty remains,
A mosaic of lessons, etched in life's refrains.
For in the letting go, a freedom is found,
To create anew on the canvas unbound.

So fear not the passing of moments untold,
For they're but threads in a tapestry bold.
Embrace the dance of time's mystical sway,
And watch as forgetting leads to a brighter day.

—— 99 ——

Embrace forgetting's gentle sway, release brings a brighter day. Memories fade, wisdom's gained, create anew, freedom unchained.

Cosmic Melody of Fated Souls

In unseen realms, where slumber's curtain's drawn,
Dreams whirl freely, with secrets yet unspoken,
A whispered truth, profound and unadorned,
"Souls don't meet by accident," it's been foretold.

Within mystical threads, destinies entwine,
Two souls converge, on paths the universe weaves,
Guided by a force beyond conscious mind,
In timeless dance, their essence interweaves.

A symphony of souls, as fate defines,
In boundless depths of ethereal space,
For every gaze exchanged, a purpose holds,
No serendipity, love's destined embrace.

In sacred union, they ignite and soar,
Infinite connections, woven with care,
Their souls aligned, forever to explore,
The truth that soul encounters are rare.

Marvel at this cosmic dance's grandeur,
Where unseen hands guide, intertwining strands,
In this sphere, beyond mere happenstance,
We find the magic that our dreams command.

So let us cherish this celestial art,
Where souls converge and destinies align,
In this vast cosmos, connected at heart,
Their cosmic melody shall ever shine.

—— **99** ——

Embrace fate's grand design, souls entwine to ascend.
Believe in rare connections, where dreams unfurl
their core in unseen realms.

CHALLENGE YOURSELF TO GROW EVERY DAY

Our hearts, like seasons, can bloom anew
after even the harshest winters.

Hidden Hurt: A Girl's Cry in Shadows

In shadows she lingers, a girl with hidden pain,
A heart heavy with burdens, yet no words to explain,
She walks through life's alleys, a solitary quest,
Afraid to show weakness, she hides her distress.

Behind her bright smile, a storm silently brews,
But she masks her emotions, as the world misconstrues,
Her tears fall in silence, in the depths of the night,
Yet she clings to her secrets, shunning the light.

In solitude, she battles the demons within,
But the weight grows heavier, the struggle more grim,
For her pride is a fortress, a barrier so high,
She's forgotten the solace that asking can supply.

Oh, girl with unspoken sorrow, don't carry alone,
Let others offer solace, their compassion be shown,
Release the shackles that bind you in despair,
Seek refuge in love, for it's others who care.

Let your voice find its wings, let your pain gently fade,
Reach out to the hands that long to aid,
In vulnerability's embrace, you shall find,
Strength to heal wounds and leave darkness behind.

No longer conceal your hurt, let the walls start to crack,
For in asking for help, you won't lose what you lack,
You're not alone on this journey, your heart need not weep,
For together we'll rise, a humanity to keep.

—— **99** ——

*In vulnerability lies strength to heal, share your
burdens, unveil your heart's shadows.
Reach out, release your pain, let compassion mend.*

In the Hands of Fate

In life's fortune, a truth so sublime,
A lesson woven through the sands of time,
Patience, dear soul, be your faithful guide,
For everything comes to you, at the right time.

When dreams elude, like stars veiled by clouds,
And despair dances, whispering doubts,
Know that destiny's rhythm is but a chime,
For everything comes to you, at the right time

When sorrow's tempests fiercely roar,
And shadows cloak the hopes you adore,
Take solace, for within life's paradigm,
Everything comes to you, at the right time.

In seasons of longing, when hearts grow weary,
And the path ahead seems rough and dreary,
Remember, dear one, amidst this paradigm,
Everything comes to you, at the right time.

Like seeds that slumber beneath winter's snow,
Life's treasures unfold, an exquisite show,
Trust in the universe, its grand design,
For everything comes to you, at the right time.

So let not impatience obscure your sight,
Embrace each moment, both day and night,
For the symphony of life, in its sublime,
Will bring everything to you, at the right time.

— 99 —

In patience and hope, your dreams align, everything comes to you, in its perfect time.

Fading Echoes of Love's Name

And, one day, his name no longer made her smile,
It whispered through the hollows of her heart,
Like a faded memory on a distant shore,
Where love's gentle waves tore them apart.

Once, his name was a melody in her ear,
A symphony of laughter and tender delight,
But now, a bitter taste lingers near,
As she gazes upon the shadows of their shattered night.

In dreams, she used to dance with his name,
Twirling through moonlit meadows of bliss,
But now it's lost in the mist of her pain,
A fleeting wisp of what they could never reminisce.

Each syllable now a thorn in her side,
A painful reminder of what they had to leave,
And though her heart longs for the love they tried,
His name brings a sorrow that's hard to conceive.

Yet, in the quiet depths of her solitude,
She searches for remnants of that fading smile,
Hoping against hope that love's interlude,
Will someday mend what has been lost for a while.

For even though his name no longer brings joy,
She holds onto the fragments of a love so pure,
And in her dreams, where hearts never deploy,
She'll cherish the memory of what once was and endure.

—————— 99 ——————

Embody pain as a testament to your heart's depth.
Let memories guide you towards healing and
enduring hope.

A Dance of Tears and Stardust

In the twilight's hush, where dreams do reside,
There dwells a girl, her heart heavy and wide.
A life loss, a wound deep, too painful to bear,
Her sorrow consumes her, leaving her gasping for air.

With each passing day, the sadness takes form,
A haunting presence, a tempestuous storm.
Her tears, like raindrops, fall on barren lands,
Aching, throbbing pain held within her hands.

Her spirit once bright, now cloaked in despair,
Her soul weeps silently, lost in the glare.
The weight of her grief, it lingers and stings,
An unyielding ache, as if hope had taken wings.

But in the darkest night, where stars gently gleam,
A flicker of solace, a shimmering beam.
Her dreams, like whispers, dance on fragile wings,
Guiding her through the night, where healing begins.

In sleep's tender embrace, her sadness finds ease,
As dreams weave a tapestry, her heart's sweet release.
With each ethereal breath, she mends her soul's core,
Unburdened, she soars, like an eagle once more.

In the realm of slumber, where beauty resides,
She finds solace and peace, where her sadness subsides.
Through dream's gentle touch, her spirit takes flight,
And she knows, in her heart, everything will be alright.

—— 🎙🎙 ——

Amid tears and stardust, embrace dreams.
Let sorrow fade. Like an eagle, soar with spirit alight.
In darkness, find light and everything's alright.

BELIEVE IN YOURSELF AND ALL THAT YOU ARE

The symphony of healing plays softly
in moments of self-acceptance.

Veiled Pages: The Silent Stories Within

In whispered echoes of a timeless tale,
Lies a chapter cloaked, beyond the pale,
Each soul, a book of secrets unspoken,
Dreams and desires silently awoken.

Every heart holds a chapter, veiled and concealed,
A world within, where emotions are revealed,
A sanctuary of hopes and silent screams,
Where shadows dance and shatter dreams.

The untold stories, they dance in the night,
Unseen by eyes, yet shining so bright,
In dreams and reveries, they come alive,
A kaleidoscope of emotions, they strive.

For deep within, where vulnerabilities reside,
There lies a treasure, buried deep inside,
A symphony of tears, laughter, and fears,
Whispered confessions, held close for years.

But take heart, dear soul, for you are not alone,
In this symphony of secrets, you've always known,
In every heart, a chapter lingers,
Unwritten tales of dreamers and singers.

So let your pen dance upon the page,
Release the words trapped in your cage,
For in the vulnerability of your voice,
You'll find solace, freedom, and rejoice.

"

Courageously delve into hidden depths.
Accept vulnerability, release words, let your heart's
symphony echo. Each chapter holds healing
and inspiring might.

The Haunting Melancholy

In dusk's grasp, a lonely girl wanders.
Her eyes mirror a thousand lost dreams.
A phantom's touch, a melancholic sigh,
Her fragile heart dances with silent agony.

She walks among the living, but feels detached,
A ghostly presence, a fleeting shade.
Invisible wounds etched upon her soul,
Her spirit lingers in the twilight's halo.

She knows the weight of a thousand grief,
Each tear a testament to her hidden strife.
Her laughter, a mere whisper in the wind,
For she has tasted death while still alive.

Her dreams, once vibrant, now bathe in gray,
A lightening of pain and yearning collide.
Her heart a broken vessel, battered and worn,
She mourns the life she once held inside.

Yet in her sadness, a peculiar beauty blooms,
Like fragile petals of a forgotten sunflower.
In her depths, the moon rays finds solace,
And the stars bear witness to her secret throes.

Oh, sad girl, may your dreams take flight,
Like delicate butterflies in a pink sky.
May hope weave its way through your soul,
And awaken the lost sparkle in your eye.

—— **,,** ——

Amid twilight's might, own your essence.
Through hope's wings, soar, painting skies with reborn
dreams. Find strength in shadows like moonlit blooms.

Like phoenix rising from ashes of despair,
strength emerges from pain's intricate layer.

YOUR
ONLY
LIMIT
IS YOU

Life's challenges are opportunities to grow.
Seize them with courage and perseverance,
for greatness lies beyond your comfort zone.

A Tale of Betrayal and Redemption

In shadows deep, where trust once bloomed,
A heart now mourns, in solitude consumed.
Betrayal's bitter sting, from friends so dear,
Whispers of envy, poisonous and near.

Once laughter danced upon the breeze,
Now tears descend, with silent pleas.
In whispered secrets, she placed her trust,
Only to find betrayal's cruel thrust.

Their envy, like a venomous vine,
Coiled around her, choking the divine.
Yet, in the crucible of despair's embrace,
She found the strength to rise, to face.

Through the shattered fragments of her soul,
She forged a path, to reclaim control.
For in the depths of grief's relentless tide,
She discovered resilience, deep inside.

Though scars may linger, etched in pain,
She knows she'll rise, to dance again.
For in the ashes of betrayal's cruel art,
She finds the fire to ignite her heart.

So let the winds of change blow strong,
For from the wreckage, she'll craft a song.
A symphony of healing, rising above,
A testament to the strength of love.

Welcome your pain as a catalyst for growth. You are not defined by those who hurt you, but by the strength with which you rise.

Bearing Truth: A Story of Pride and Pain

In the depths of her soul, grief finds its home,
A torrent of sorrow, relentless and lone.
Once intertwined, their spirits danced as one,
Now severed by fate, their bond undone.

She mourns not just loss, but the betrayal's sting,
A soulmate turned stranger, love's shattered wing.
Her heart, a canvas of memories turned to dust,
As the echoes of his anger leave her heart crushed.

Each word a dagger, each glance a wound,
His resentment a tempest, her peace marooned.
She reaches out, her hand trembling with despair,
But he turns away, his pride a fortress, unaware.

Oh, the agony of unspoken words unsaid,
A chasm widening, where love once tread.
She bears her truth, honest and raw,
But his pride, a barrier, an insurmountable flaw.

Yet still she persists, in the face of his disdain,
Hoping against hope, for healing's gentle rain.
For in her heart, a flicker of hope remains,
That one day forgiveness may break these chains.

So let her tears flow, like rivers to the sea,
For in her sorrow lies her humanity.
And though his resentment may tear her apart,
She'll rise from the ashes, with a resilient heart.

Embrace your pain as a testament to your humanity, and trust that healing will come. Keep faith, for every trial is a stepping stone towards renewal and inner strength.

RISE ABOVE THE STORM AND YOU WILL FIND THE SUNSHINE

Nurture self-love like a gardener caring for delicate blossoms, for within the petals resides the core of enduring strength.

Defiant Spirit

In the depths of her soul, she battles unseen foes,
Anxiety's whispers, grief's relentless throes.
Yet she stands, a force, unyielding and bold,
Defiant against shadows, against all that's told.

Through tear-stained nights and endless fears,
She walks with courage, despite mocking jeers.
For within her burns a flame, fierce and bright,
Guiding her through the darkest of night.

Through the tempest of sorrow, she forges her way,
Her heart heavy with loss, yet she'll not sway.
For within her beats a spirit, fierce and bold,
Guided by a light, a truth to behold.

Though storms may rage and darkness may fall,
She rises unbroken, answering the call.
With each step forward, she defies the night,
Her courage a beacon, her resolve a light.

Those once close, now plotting, their envy revealed,
But undeterred, to her truth she'll wield.
For she knows within, there's a power untold,
A strength that transcends, a love that unfolds.

Let the rain pour, let the winds howl,
In her heart, hope reigns, a steady growl.
For she is the keeper of her own destiny,
A warrior of the soul, in her, find serenity.

—— 🙹🙹 ——

Unleash your inner strength, and let hope's steady
growl guide you through.
You are capable of rising strong.

Cycles of Grace: A Reflection on Kindness

In the tapestry of life, kindness threads the needle,
Stitching together hearts with a gentle touch,
Each act a ripple in the vast ocean of existence,
Where compassion reigns and souls find solace.

Forgiveness, a balm for wounds unseen,
Heals the scars of bitterness and resentment,
In its embrace, we find liberation,
A release from the chains that bind us to the past.

Yet arrogance, a poison coursing through veins,
Blinds us to the humanity in each other's eyes,
Inflating egos until they burst with hubris,
Leaving behind a wreckage of broken relationships.

Pride, the silent architect of our downfall,
Builds walls where bridges should stand,
Its bricks laid with ignorance and folly,
Separating us from the beauty of empathy.

But in the end, humility whispers its wisdom,
A gentle reminder of our shared frailty,
Guiding us back to the path of grace,
Where kindness and forgiveness pave the way.

Let us then, with open hearts, choose to be kind,
To forgive, and leave arrogance behind.
For in humility's embrace, we find our worth,
And in kindness, we unearth the treasures of the earth.

———— **99** ————

Let kindness be your compass, forgiveness mend the fabric of our souls, and may humility guide us to embrace our shared humanity with genuine love.

Amidst the storms within,
remember clouds part,
and sunlight finds its way.

A journey through shadows reveals our might.

EVERY DAY IS A FRESH START

mental
health
matters

Dear Reader,

As I close the pages of Rhymes of the Heart, I am struck by the intricate tapestry of human emotions that intricately weaves through our lives. However, beyond the mere words etched upon these pages lies a powerful call to action—an invitation to embark on a profound journey of self-discovery and healing.

As you approach the conclusion of this book, I implore you not to let the journey end here. Instead, let it serve as a catalyst for your personal transformation through engaging in the mental health exercises provided.

Take hold of your pen, and embark on your own creative odyssey. Allow the prompts and suggestions nestled within these pages to ignite your imagination and prompt you to express yourself in ways previously unimagined.

Take a moment to reflect and inscribe three things you are willing to release, initiating your healing process right now.

1.

2.

3.

May you summon the courage from within to embrace your pain as an integral facet of your humanity, understanding that even amidst the darkest of moments, a light of hope persists, guiding us towards healing and renewal.

WRITE A POEM INSPIRED BY A SIGNIFICANT EMOTION OR EXPERIENCE IN YOUR LIFE.

Tip: Allow yourself to play with language and imagery as you explore your inner world through poetry to release your emotions.

CREATE A VISUAL REPRESENTATION OF YOUR INNER SELF. USE COLORS, SHAPES, AND TEXTURES TO EXPRESS YOUR EMOTIONS AND THOUGHTS.

Tip: Don't worry about creating a masterpiece, focus on the process of self-expression.

WRITE A SHORT STORY OR NARRATIVE THAT EXPLORES THEMES OF RESILIENCE AND OVERCOMING ADVERSITY. CREATE CHARACTERS WHO NAVIGATE CHALLENGES AND DISCOVER THEIR INNER STRENGTH.

Tip: Draw inspiration from your own experiences or invent fictional worlds where characters embark on journeys of self-discovery.

EMPOWER YOURSELF WITH DAILY AFFIRMATIONS BELOW.

1. *I am worthy of love and kindness, both from others and from myself.*
2. *I embrace my emotions fully, knowing that they are valid and a natural part of being human.*
3. *I trust in my ability to overcome challenges and grow stronger with each experience.*
4. *I release any negative thoughts or beliefs that no longer serve me, replacing them with positivity and optimism.*
5. *I am resilient and capable of weathering life's storms with grace and courage.*
6. *I am enough just as I am, and I deserve to take up space in this world.*
7. *I choose to focus on the present moment, finding joy and gratitude in the little things.*
8. *I honor my boundaries and prioritize self-care, knowing that my well-being is important.*
9. *I forgive myself for past mistakes and allow myself to move forward with compassion and grace.*
10. *I am deserving of happiness, and I trust in my ability to create a life filled with meaning and fulfillment.*

Remember, you are never alone.
Keep shining brightly.

With love,
Sheena.

ABOUT THE AUTHOR

Emerging at the age of 29, Fathmath Sheena embodies a dynamic spirit, originating from the breathtaking Maldives, a small yet captivating nation nestled in the Indian Ocean. Her literary journey commenced amidst the backdrop of personal loss, as both her mother and the love of her life passed away unexpectedly, leaving an indelible mark on her life. Fueled by empathy and a desire to inspire positivity, she embarked on a path of writing with the noble intention of reigniting faith and fostering a deeper understanding of mental well-being.

This inaugural book publication marks a significant milestone in her journey.

Stay connected on social media: @fathmathsheena, @sheenasrhymes

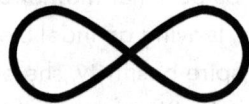

POETRY IN MOTION

Unlock the verses, embrace the art, through grief, through pain, hope's sweet start, its journeys through the mind's brave chart.

Rhymes of the Heart is a collection of poems that delves into the depths of human emotions. With themes of grief, pain, and hope, these verses traverse the intricate landscapes of mental health.

Through introspection and vulnerability, the poems inspire readers to embrace their pain as an essential part of their humanity. This book serves as a guiding light, reminding us that even in the darkest moments, hope shines through, leading us to healing and renewal. At the end of the book, readers will find creative mental health exercises to further aid in their healing journey.

To feel pain is a part of being human!

FATHMATH SHEENA

www.ingramcontent.com/pod-product-compliance
Lightning Source LLC
Chambersburg PA
CBHW072009060426
42446CB00042B/2275